SLEEPING IN A FIELD

SLEEPING IN A FIELD

TRIIN PAJA

WOLFSON PRESS
2025

Copyright © 2025 by Triin Paja.
Designed by Sky Santiago.
All rights reserved. First edition.

ISBN: ISBN: 978-1-950066-19-3

Wolfson Press
Master of Liberal Studies Program
Indiana University South Bend
1700 Mishawaka Avenue
South Bend, Indiana 46634-7111
WolfsonPress.com

Contents

Foreword   vii
Journal of Solitude   1
To Touch, Not to Wound   2
In the Vineyard   3
Fostering   4
Portrait of Old Animals   5
Mother Fox   6
Bone River   7
Winter Farm   8
Wing Diary   9
Another Earth   10
Clearcutting   11
Trees at Dusk   12
Sleeping in a Forest   14
Another Beginning   15
Jar of Feathers   16
Wolf Crane, Lilac Moon   17
Whale Song   18
Sleeping in a Field   19
Luule   21
Riverlight   23
Remembering Winter   24
Daughters   25
Predawn   26
Wordless on the Shore   27
Barley   28
Fire Preservation   29
Hypostasis   30
Small Offerings   31
Acknowledgments   33

Foreword

If *Sleeping in a Field* does one thing, it showcases poet Triin Paja's descriptive powers at their best. Her mission is to celebrate nature's wonder and exquisite beauty without ignoring its menacing and violent shadows. She enters her poems through language that is stunning and elegant. If you're lucky enough to remember an unplugged childhood, Paja's poems will rekindle what might be diminished or lost by giving voice to what many of us recognize but can seldom articulate.

When we read the poems in this collection, we are reminded of nature's restorative powers—both physically and emotionally—because Paja is wholly immersed in the natural world and does not draw distinctions between herself and other living things, but rather sees herself as part of a larger whole. In the opening poem, "Journal of Solitude," she says that she "chose fields instead of children / and stored [her] love in the snowy drawers // of a whooper swan." The beloved field is indeed the central image in these poems, and, by extension, what a field contains. Birds and bones consume the speaker's attention. The force of her seeing—and the sheer force of her language—becomes a sacred act. In "Whale Song," she writes, "the oil red sun // lifts with the brass seabirds. / hear the axe-silver sea humming." She may not have chosen motherhood herself, but she watches mothers in the wild commit violence in the service of their young, a natural process she does not shy away from: the mother fox "unbutton[s] the belly of a hare," and a seal pup is "unraveled by seagulls and crows," actions that are "not cruel." Bones are what living things are ultimately reduced to, but there is no fretting here about inevitable death or the decay of the body. In fact, in one poem, a young girl uses a moose bone for a doll, and after her death, the girl's bones return to earth to serve as "toys" for the animals. Unlike Louise Glück who used nature to reflect death and sadness, Paja is buoyed by its rhythms and cycles, and she balances mortality and loss with living and rejuvenation. Glück's poems are no less powerful from the vantage point of suburbia, but in these poems Paja's feet are planted firmly in the mire. If there is pain, it is human pain; mothers are damaged physically by toiling on the farm, by engaging in backbreaking labor. Whether human or animal, mothers bear the brunt of caring for offspring and maintaining stasis in a harsh environment. In "Luule" she remembers:

> as a child, I washed my yellow hair in a yellow bowl
>   pouring water from a glass jar   over my head
>
> cotton shirts, grey wool   hanging above me:
>   the laundry washed in the same yellow bowl

For Paja, an impoverished childhood does not mean an impoverished existence. Time and time again her gaze fixes on the sky, the river, stones, cattle, bones, birds, bees, trees, and flowers, as if these things are touchstones or talismans that provide spiritual ballast. The images in her poems are not confined to sight. "You must come to this / blue garden," she says in "Wolf Crane, Lilac Moon,"

> when the moon
> when the moon—
> the moon will bury lilacs in our skin
>
> wind moving the weeds for it cannot sing
>   a raven coughing above   plaited to a branch
>
> swallows sounding
>   their silvery keys unlocking doors

Language can bolster the imagination and guide us to places we may have thought were lost. This poet shows us some of those places, and it might be wise to go searching ourselves for what the world offers us each day. In "Predawn," she confesses, "mud was beautiful to me," and

> I felt nearer to the intelligence of crows,
> to the beauty of stones,
> than to my body
>
> [. . .]
>
> I heard the heartbeats of owls and hares.

In the title poem, Paja says, "writing becomes memory." The act of writing may force one to remember, but that phrase is too limiting. What she also suggests is that memory has a more expansive role, especially for the writer, by taking one out of the self and into new realms where magic occurs and simple acts shine brightly. For example, in "Fostering," she says, "a woman walks / so slowly, as if her body // held the weight of war letters." Paja elevates the ordinary, and we too are lifted.

The shift in modern times from a close connection to nature to the comfort and convenience of indoor life has been building for decades. Experts have warned that this lack of connection will deaden our senses, but they are mildly dismissed or outright ignored. Contributing, perhaps, are the endless news cycles which bring dire news from across the globe of not only nature's destructive force but of the dangers that lurk in the woods or other desolate areas. These poems will restore our faith in nature's abundant gifts and also the balance we may have lost. We are richer for having been exposed to Triin Paja's radiant mind. She is a poet to watch.

Nancy Botkin
South Bend, Indiana

It is better to say, "I am suffering," than to say, "This landscape is ugly."

—Simone Weil, *Gravity and Grace*

Journal of Solitude

that I chose fields instead of children
and stored my love in the snowy drawers

of a whooper swan
has not ended my reaching for you

but I must often be dew-drenched, silent, ajar.

my reaching for you—
reading together,

your hand holding
a book, your other hand holding

my hand, removed only to turn a page.

even within the poem I am trying
to shelter you

but I have been a creature of sorrow
like other children,

pining to be a small sound,
a creak or a creek.

for I have shuddered below
a spruce branch,

lowered to hands and knees
to eat the snow,

for my throat grew sore
whistling to indecipherable birds

for, thereafter, speaking felt like betrayal.

To Touch, Not to Wound

what I held was whole winters listening to families   scream from lack
           women's wrists bruised into cornflowers
                         the beer-sweet breath of children

what I held was cold and craving, tensed when the women appeared
       in their windows   staring into a Soviet mythology

of rust-petaled factories
        of perfume drank as alcohol
              where the only sun   was the luminous concrete

what I held was mother's silvery rope of hair
              held cowslip and dandelion
                          coltsfoot powdering our hands

what I held were days   gathering their voices   weeping by their stoves

what I held was absence becoming weather becoming sound
                      church towers among khrushchyovkas

        what I wanted to hold was every name, every name of
somewhere-woman wrapping a skull in a lace cloth
            somewhere-woman preparing a meal for a photograph

        what I wanted to hold turned into sky, her hair turned into sky
her voice turned into sky, the voice saying:
          I will leave the earth   as a bird leaves a branch

In the Vineyard

the bed, narrow as a coffin,
creaks like a tame swan

when I wake,
famished, in the night.

I pick grapes from the vineyard
with bees gone delirious

from rotting fruit.

below a leaf, a quiescent insect
dreams

of when it was liquid
in its jade chrysalis, a memory

as impossible as my own arrival:

a muddy loaf in mother's
magnolia hands.

I ask, like the bees,
if memory is always blighted.

if beneath this chamfron of
maturity,
        manners,

I am still a stupidly generous child,
a cursed animal

lurking in the vines
with my one startling joy, a desire to live.

Fostering

waking, I find only the sun,
an animal frozen in a winter cloud.

outside, a small boy looks
to a seagull crying on a chimney.

he could be a man but as he looks
to a seagull in a city of seagulls

he is a child. a woman walks
so slowly, as if her body

held the weight of war letters.
you know nights are unkind

even if lit by the moon's candelabra
so I hide the scraps of paper

saying six cygnets were fed to death
by good-hearted citizens. alone,

I remember two village boys entering
my home, scattering berries

on the floor, crushing them. alone,
I wonder what evokes the cruelty of boys.

the cries of the seagulls stir you,
the birthmarks on your back

tremble with sensuality.

on the table,
the wilted necks of dried poppies.

Portrait of Old Animals

i.

I carve a cross for a bird's grave
as the cold wind sings terrible songs

into the ears of feral kittens.
I believed the wind was the wingspan

of a ghost, but it is only the wind,
the way the earth is only earth.

I recall my first bird, a kaleidoscopic bird,
an anarchy of light. then someone said

bird, and the bird attained its birdness.
afterwards, it was impossible to see them.

ii.

on this earth, I entered a forest
and crushed a clover with my breathing.

on this earth, someone collects the frozen feet
of elephants. another fills a freezer

with tiger cubs. on this earth, I see a grave
in each beetle-ghosted rose

and never see the bird, the elephant,
the tiger. over the forest floor,

twigs fall in the shape of crosses.

Mother Fox

mother fox, you unbutton the belly of a hare
in a rapeseed field,
the belly with leverets inside
listless as laundry folded by careful hands,

and stand in hunger-glitched brightness,
and warn:

*I wish you such hunger the moon will seem an onion,
ore in your belly,
a wing grown inward, a mildewed ribcage.*

then lapwings heave into view growing into small suns.

*

I smell the carcass of a seal pup by the shore
unraveled by seagulls and crows.
the sea is not cruel. their beaks are not cruel.

no cruelty in the mother fox
whose love gently
then fiercely gnaws. a child

may be an anthem of silt and wound.
a mother's flesh hardens into her son's
breastplate.
she pelts her skin

for her daughter's winter.

*

often I see you
at dusk
where I stumble into the hazel
of your one eye, and the blue of the other, blind.

a bird perches on a skull.
mother, I am your cursed city; you are a knot of dark devotions.

Bone River

tonight, the sheep hum
for the bones of their young.
the wind's wolf pack howls.
a woman gathers herbs
for her own animal ghosts.
in November, she gives me
a box of apples lined with
gardening articles.
swallows circle the dusk
in her eyes. in July,
the thin boughs of her legs
sway in a river
lit with globeflowers.
no one hears how a lamb slips
but the mother. no one hears
how a body walks into a river
as into a room, closing the door.
as a girl, the woman's voice
was a lilac bush. we cannot ask
how the leaves caught fire.
bones turn to stones
in the river.
sheep haunt this water.
the woman enters
its blue breast, not as
a body, but as a requiem,
forming a wreath of bones
in the bleating water.

Winter Farm

the walk to the farm, the glow
of the frozen path, then swallows,

hay rot, calves. the hay wounds
on her hands. to know her pain,

a mother's. in the corridor,
a dead bee-light,

scent of milk powder.
to know the axe silvering

into frozen haystacks,
to know her pain, a mother's:

a child carrying a sheep
in her lap,

a child building
a shelter of birch twigs.

she named the bones
in the slaughterhouse,

each of the hundreds of animals

had a name. we brushed our hands
over their rose tongues.

in the half-limbed light
of the winter farm

the rattle of chains.

Wing Diary

in the field where crickets sound
like rocking chairs

hidden in rye
is the western marsh harrier

her yellow orb-like eyes
and arched bill

imply claw and clamor
but she is a tarnished key

that opens the door of the field
the room we cannot fathom

*

the cries of the seagull:
as if she carries the sea with her

a bird as grey as remorse
in peacock dusk

when she reaches me
her wing-light covers me

like an eggshell

*

at first, only the wind
prying open the mouth of the lake

then the crane howling
floods the leaf-floor

the crane, the strangest river
sings the sky-path to the blue house

where we will sleep together

Another Earth

there were no birds
even if the trees creaked like birds
even if the dawn implied the perpetuity
of a sensual sky
as I saw a bird-shadow on a wall
and awoke to an earth
   iridescent, unbeautiful
as a seabird turned from gull to crow
with tarred oil.

I buried a small bird
and climbed a tree calcified with lichen.
the wind began to turn my hair grey.
I was not a child. I learned
we are also like the river
for we cannot return.

I loved a bird, but it was like seeing
a lover in the sea, but you
are at the bottom, you see his belly,
the sun above. then there were
no birds, even as rail tracks
glowed in the dark
with the sheen of ravens
and grass grew tall as geese.

Clearcutting

in Latvia, a charcoal wolf,
with fur like smoke,

rescues her cubs
bundled under felled trees,

masked in the emerald potsherds

from trees tall as lighthouses,
now stumps, marred root, nest dust.

one by one, she carries
her children, grasping them

gently with her young-moon teeth.

she could be a silver-haired mother
digging for her children

in a bombed city.

the wind is the largest room
she knows

and it is growing.

Trees at Dusk

I listened to the forest
which was not

a forest. snow,
yellow

like the yellowed lace curtains
of childhood.

weeds thinned to a murmur.

a black woodpecker trembled
after the logging—

how to make a nest in the sky?

we harvest
the sea, the air.

we harvest
as if we are famished

but you have steeped yourself
in the fragrances

of our markets and windowsills
and know our pretense.

you alight upon
the train's whistle:

a sound so deep it reaches,
with its dark hand,

into the earth.

moose tracks
spell further laments.

my grief ought to be green.

I ought to hear when
a fox barks

wearily

telling us to leave, telling us

here there is nothing to hurt you,
nothing for you to love.

Sleeping in a Forest

I buried a small tortoiseshell in a matchbox
to soothe my hands
in the parched field. a white stork

lifted, eager to puncture
the sky's rain-swollen belly.
the body is soothed by strangeness

they trust. I do not speak
of the river-strangeness, where the animal
loses its voice first—

no. hear me. though you love
the river's darkness
do not sleep in its arms.

then I went into
a small forest
the breadth of a cuckoo's call.

I felt full, as if I had devoured
bowls of soup
and the only hand on my eyelids was sleep.

and in my dream the trees grew back.

remember.
there was a forest.
my mother cut her hand there

picking orange milkcaps
between its mossy legs.
the trees rustled

their sleeves
trusting us
with their hearts that cried resin.

Another Beginning

I ran into the forest to hear the cuckoo.
the earth was boar-bruised,

the roots marred,
raw. boar,

I also prefer to terrify
than be ankle-shackled by longing.

then the cuckoo called out.

there is a field inside the bird,
and the idea of time.

like the bird, I want to inherit nothing
from mirrors.

I want to run into the forest,
again, again—

there is honor in waiting,
but also a certain death:

wake up, beloved.

I ran into the forest. I sent,
foolishly, a kiss to the cuckoo.

I adored my foolishness.

I smelled a twig of jasmine
and my face fell into it:

yes, death is in me, but it is not my name.
I unfurl in all directions—

this has no end. becoming is a river.

Jar of Feathers

I have not forgotten your city
        where I smiled when you stole sweets in the streets
                where the wind cobwebbed itself around all, its birds
    parrots and hummingbirds

         I know I am not there when I count the empty stork nests
on chimneys, electricity posts

      it is summer when cracked concrete opens in dandelions
when the earth is textured in hill mustard

      you say, there is only dust and sun where you live, only summer
I say, for many years it was believed
              swallows hibernated underwater

an image of fish and swallows pulled in a fishnet
        from a lake   I say, it was believed birds migrated on the moon

you say, there is only dust, and sun
             I say, a lake full of swallows, a moon white with birds—

I have not forgotten your city, it held your skin
        warm as tealeaves at the bottom of a cup
                I see a field and call it your hair

you say, there is more dust to you than flesh
    I say, all I have is a small lake shining white with the bones of cats and cattle
              at the bottom

I say, it is winter here, birds freeze into lakes,
        women the color of lichen carry bread in bare hands

it is winter here, I have only skin feathered in memory,
              yellow fields under the rosy underbellies of clouds

you say, you have gathered fruit, bruised and bright,
                but holding, carrying it to me

      I say, bird, and sky

Wolf Crane, Lilac Moon

I've begun to call the cranes wolves—
I awake in their grey howling

    I want to show you my earth
        where I pluck rhubarbs
  from an abandoned garden

      you must come to this
    blue garden
      when the moon
      when the moon—
the moon will bury lilacs in our skin

wind moving the weeds for it cannot sing
      a raven coughing above   plaited to a branch

swallows sounding
    their silvery keys unlocking doors

  in Japanese folklore, cranes turn into women
      they pluck their feathers in secret
    scar themselves
      to weave dazzling fabrics—

  too many birds
  yet I must write in feather and hollow bone

      construct a sky
not the human habitat of word

      I did not want to say human
  but bird, bird, bird

to show you a winged garden
    and not say oil spill, window, rifle

    in the end, the crane-women return to the sky
  I meant to say

  a bird may die
of heart failure
    if you place it in the lotus of your palm—

Whale Song

I awake to the grey eyes of the sea
everywhere looking. this is not the ship

where oil was extracted
from the cavities of whale heads.

our lamps are not fish-perfumed.
our hands not softened with whale soap.

instead, seagulls sail in an arc of hunger.
small wind-bodies knead the water.

a lighthouse on a few stones
dappled white with swan excrement

is not fuelled by whale oil.
the sea, crooked and creaking,

is not that sea, and is. our ship floats
like a slayed whale. when it turns,

a stuffed seagull wearing a seashell necklace
rings softly. the oil red sun

lifts with the brass seabirds.
hear the axe-silver sea humming:

a wave slams against the ship
as a whale slams into the boat of oil miners.

my bruises heal
growing green like the leaves of water lilies—

but there is no end to the chaos of a whale calf
trying to suckle on a vessel

carrying the skeletal moraines of mother.

Sleeping in a Field

I.

        in a dream moths thud into my body
                            mistaking me for light

II.

the way to the water:
    a one-eared yellow cat,
        beach roses, swans like bones in the air.

then it was only the hanging moss of your damp hair,
the sea's painting of hysteria behind you.

no one asking who will bring us water.
    no one stopping the soft prayer of your hands
        breaking up bread, oranges.

we did not speak of her, though we saw faces of girls
in dusk-blushed rocks.

only later, in a letter, did we say. writing becomes memory.

the wine bottle fell
to form a bazaar of lanterns. what could we say?

the sea-wind eats our words, the way particles of light
begin to fall into night's mouth.

it didn't mean absence of thought. someone touching
her long, unwashed hair. like coarse wheat.

it was only something hushed in our village.
a girl fell asleep in a field and then it was blood

brushed on wheat, the sound of tractors humming,
the white feathers of sunlight falling, and falling.

Luule

as a child, I washed my yellow hair in a yellow bowl
        pouring water from a glass jar   over my head

cotton shirts, grey wool   hanging above me:
         the laundry washed in the same yellow bowl

thoughts of summer   small moons of dandelion heads
      ready to spit their seeds   cottonwood snow   wilted hay

in the awareness of cow bones in moonlight
                  the hay smelled of suffering

~

you shepherded cows   the shed roof where we lay, the cows
        blooming in dew-bright fields

your name meant poetry. your parents, deaf, did not speak
      but sang, like cranes:
             a river of echoes, a haunted church

your mother's long hair the color of faded coins
                we were braided into it

~

the poverty of childhood does not become
             the poverty of memory   memory
spreads as a sea, floods all, clouds all

           it is not you who speaks, who dreams
   it is the sea   pearl-heavy inside you

~

now, only if my body becomes a scythe, cutting through the weeds,
      may I locate the gardens, the fields   beyond

~

       I want to believe the sky is still offered to you
  a sky bleached by white storks

the cows are other cows. there is no room inside us

                    to fit the long limbs we had as children

when you look back
        are the fields burning; have they turned to storks, to churches—

Riverlight

the sky is precisely you: the ribs
of a starved boy.

the sky is burial water
and when we searched for drowned cattle

we looked above. we looked,
scarcely seeing, as one-eyed dogs.

the childhood cattle never drowned:
the river drowned in them.

still, the sky is precisely you, the sky
is your mouth haunting my mouth.

hear the old animal
eating the river's moldered water lilies—

I have also eaten out of the bowl
of such loneliness: wild strawberries

amid weed-eaten graves. you do not reply
for you are already in a house of ferns

and the river flows more quietly.
barnacles blanket crystallized skulls

or stones. the sky opens again
and it is precisely you:

a torn photograph of your shoulder blade.

and the cattle below and above,
and the riverlight flowing into

and out of their bodies.

Remembering Winter

I hold dark tea in your ruined city.
desire, a pitcher of wildflowers between us.

the air, weeded with night. your heart,
mosque-blue. I try to articulate, and fail,

the sadness of cows drinking from
a thawed puddle, a box of winter cabbage,

the dry, cold hour of home.
I hold the dark tea. I am trying to learn

holding without desire. here, rice boils in broth.
here, you give me lemons, a jar of tahini,

you say, bring them to your mother—
but there is a field burning with winter,

a winter of water damage, of potatoes only.
my mother's name is the last rowan berry,

lilac wilt, the blushed cheeks of
red currant juice brewed late summer.

I hold the dark tea. I kiss your hands, your
kind hands, the marble of which hasn't,

yet, cracked. I speak. I speak, then.
once in childhood, a man with

a horse carriage. once, many times,
I stumbled on a rotting moose. the sunset

lit its lanterns over blackened cow parsley.
my mother's name is the sound

of the river freezing.
winter never left without bones.

Daughters

I knew an old, lonely girl
whose doll was a moose bone.

she lay against
raveled raven-dark roots,

in the hollows left by deer
and carried back her own blossoming.

in the house,
pearling still meant perishing.

in the house, bread was broken
and then bodies.

her spruce-wild voice
was mangled into sweetness.

in the house, the sun was a rotting apricot.
beyond the house, the sun

was generous and she ate
the crumbs of the sun like the birds,

saying *father, father.*

her body unfurled only beyond visibility
and so the forest became

her resting place, her bones became
dolls for bears and otters.

later, I heard her father say:
I always loved daughters more than sons—

how he cried for two years, every day,
after her passing. how he opens

his small, yellow bible, and disappears.

Predawn

like a young child, I never knew the concept of ugly.
I was child-like, cursed and gentle,
and the mud was beautiful to me. snail and flint.

I felt nearer to the intelligence of crows,
to the beauty of stones,
than to my body.

one morning I stood on a river stone
rusted and shaped like the helmet of drowned soldier
and saw a dark bird

carrying smoldering sticks
to start a fire.
I heard the heartbeats of owls and hares.

I danced until I was a staircase
spiraling into a howl.
the fire was a hunger, a mouth.

it smelled like the fruit trees
that for weeks had been singing sugar and rot.

each of my blood cells singing or longing
while the forest flamed
and the trees sounded like so many crows laughing.

I burned, but my heart did not become
burnt bread. the fire never ate
my love.

the fire told me what I always knew.
to stop telling yourself the story of your life.
to be attentive now

to the strange world without you.

Wordless on the Shore

seashells break into broken nails
on the shore
where a village drunk sits
by the water's
salt-crocheted edge.
there was a time when
I played with his daughter.
she liked the sweet taste of beer.
we had lived for a decade.
the father read and read until
his pain grew tender
like a boy's nettle-blistered ankles
running in a field.
then the village library was closed
and he drank until his house
was an empty jam jar,
until his window
was only the wide mouth
of water, until his daughter grew thin
like tea sediment
then disappeared entirely.
he drinks. shadows, arboreal and human,
run towards him like horses.
he is more horse than horseman
but once, his palms curved into psalms
humming safety.
he was a boy once, nothing wormed
in the polished fruit
of his flesh.
a crow lifts from the shore.
the crow's cawing chars
the air, rousing him.
neither knows beauty that is not violent.

Barley

at night, after charting the river-sound,
the poor come out to eat the barley porridge
sacrificed on a stone. a breath surfaces
as a snowberry afloat on the water.
after pulling a drowned horse
from the river, they wonder if weight
will ever be familiar. it takes several men
to pull out a horse. at night, several men
lay beside a woman, and her bed is a riverbed.
at dawn, the sun is a gold tooth
pulled from a dead woman's mouth.
they say the dead look like marble.
the softness in her mouth, remains of barley.

Fire Preservation

if you ask me where I am going
I am going where a birch without leaves

no longer resembles the starved. I am going
into the wind. afterwards,

I will still be going.

if you ask me more, then the world
will answer you: the hills will burn,

a song will fossilize
in the ambers of flame.

it is not a rocking chair that will burn,
nor a violin or a leather-bound ode,

but the tulip weight of mice bones,
an indigo wingspan, air

incensed with charred wolf fur.

if I lay under a tree bleeding with cherries,
I am too far. if the heat is a casket of light,

I am too near. if a child with old legs
is singing, I am near, near.

the fire bellows river absence.
a river is how the land heals itself.

one may cry to the fire: *land, land*—
and the fire will answer:

*o child sacrifice, leper, widow, o witch
burning, o you, I am still only your child.*

Hypostasis

Have you thanked God for this failure already?
– Arvo Pärt

at dusk, in a garden, a woman tells me
her child had blonde hair, like mine.
the air is so blue, the greenhouse
is a mosque. the garden's belly

is full of weeds and the weight
of a dead daughter's hair.
you must learn tenderness
that is not erotic, nor asking.

a violin plays in the heart of a girl
until she is touched. at dusk,
she desires a daughter's face:
a deer heaving a mythology until

it becomes a skeleton. we kneel
with her bones in the nettles.
the nettles do not sting us.
they do not sing to us either.

what is buried here, animal
and child, drinks the mist water
dripping from apples. impassively,
night purges all color, bird, leaf, hair.

grass murmurs the hushed prayers
of caged saints: to say a daughter's
name as gently. even this becomes oil
for the lantern of our poor earth.

Small Offerings

to know what a soul is: holding a small hand,
braiding another's shuddering hair.

the soul longs, suffers,
for to have said too much

is anguish, as if one has failed to guard
one's vital, vulnerable gift.

it is better to speak
the love language of carrying tea

to each other (it becomes a world for me),
to live on the cusp of becoming-light with you.

I consider this while coloring our home
with music, though I am haunted

by latest words:

another plastic bag of kittens hung on a signpost
(I take my cat into my arms gently, gently),

birds shattering against billboards,
choking on airborne gases,

the sulfur of New Year's festivities.

roots, like twigs, coil into nest-shapes
to home the birds I bury.

I have carried enough tea
to fill our bathtub. where our souls bathe.

where the soul says I no longer desire
to be the flower in a vase—

I wish to be the water now, the vessel, the world.

Acknowledgments

I am grateful to the editors of the following journals where some of these poems first appeared, sometimes in slightly different form:

32 Poems: "Wing Diary"
The Adroit Journal: "Remembering Winter"
Apple Valley Review: "Trees at Dusk"
Arc Poetry Magazine: "Barley"
Bennington Review: "In the Vineyard"
Denver Quarterly: "Wolf Crane, Lilac Moon"
Driftwood: "Fire Preservation"
Entropy: "To Touch, Not to Wound"
decomP: "Jar of Feathers"
Frontier Poetry: "Hypostasis"
The Glacier: "Mother Fox"
isacoustic: "Luule"
The Journal: "Wordless on the Shore" (republished in *Poetry Daily*)
Pleiades: "Bone River" and "Whale Song"
Prairie Schooner: "Sleeping in a Field"
Rattle's Poets Respond: "Clearcutting"
Redivider: "Another Earth"
Reliquiae Journal: "Winter Farm," "Daughters," and "Portrait of Old Animals"
Southword: "Another Beginning"
Verseville: "Riverlight" and "Fostering"

Triin Paja lives in a small village in rural Estonia. She is the author of three collections of poetry in Estonian and a recipient of the Värske Rõhk Poetry Award, the Betti Alver Literary Award, and the Juhan Liiv Prize for Poetry. Her English poetry has received two Pushcart Prizes and has appeared in such journals as *Poetry, The Glacier, Prairie Schooner, The Adroit Journal, Apple Valley Review,* and *Entropy. Sleeping in a Field* is her first book publication in English. Her poetry has been translated into Czech, Finnish, Russian, Lithuanian, Latvian, and Slovenian. Paja is a member of the Estonian Writers' Union.

www.ingramcontent.com/pod-product-compliance
Lightning Source LLC
Chambersburg PA
CBHW021001090426
42736CB00010B/1420